Recognizing the Stranger

Also by Isabella Hammad

Enter Ghost
The Parisian

Recognizing the Stranger

On Palestine and Narrative

Isabella Hammad

Black Cat
New York

From Mahmoud Darwish's *Journal of an Ordinary Grief*, translated from Arabic
by Ibrahim Muhawi, Archipelago Books, 2010. Reprinted with permission
from the publisher.

FIRST EDITION

Published simultaneously in Canada
Printed in Canada

The interior of this book was designed by Norman E. Tuttle
of Alpha Design & Composition
This book was set in 12.25-pt. Abobe Calson by
Alpha Design & Composition in Pittsfield, NH.

First Grove Atlantic paperback edition: September 2024

Library of Congress Cataloging-in-Publication data is available for this title.

ISBN 978-0-8021-6392-9
eISBN 978-0-8021-6402-5

Black Cat
an imprint of Grove Atlantic
154 West 14th Street
New York, NY 10011

Distributed by Publishers Group West

groveatlantic.com

24 25 26 27   10 9 8 7 6 5 4 3 2 1

"Gaza does not propel people to cool contemplation; rather she propels them to erupt and collide with the truth."

—Mahmoud Darwish

This lecture was originally delivered on September 28, 2023, as the Edward W. Said Memorial Lecture at Columbia University organized by the Society of Fellows and the Heyman Center for the Humanities.

Recognizing the Stranger

When I was wondering what to talk about in this lecture, I started thinking about Edward Said and lateness as a point of departure. Then I went back to his early book *Beginnings*. And then I decided after all that I preferred to start in the middle, and more specifically that I wanted to talk about the middle of narratives—their turning points, which I'll relate to the shifting narrative shape of the Palestinian struggle in its global context.

It's difficult, in life, to pinpoint with any real sense of confidence where a turning point is located. As Said said of beginnings—whether of texts, epochs, or ideas—the turning point is likewise a human construction, something we

1

identify in retrospect. We look back on our lives, or on the course of history, and according to the shape of the particular narrative we are telling we can say—ah, see, that is how the course of the story developed, and that was a key node when everything changed. We can see these moments quite clearly from the vantage of hindsight; we can assert the significance of past events with relative confidence. In the Bulgarian writer Georgi Gospodinov's 2020 novel *Time Shelter*, the narrator notes that history becomes history only after the fact: "Most likely," he says, speaking of the beginning of World War II, "1939 did not exist in 1939, there were just mornings when you woke up with a headache, uncertain and afraid." But if we cannot always know the significance of the moment *in* the moment, it is also true that our moment, the one in which we now live, feels like one of chronic "crisis": political, economic, and climate crises besiege us, along with other existential crises posed by the exponential development of artificial intelligence, and the recurring nightmare of nuclear war. In narrative time, the crisis should suggest the encroachment of the end, even if, in real life, the end is a receding horizon. The flow of history always exceeds the narrative frames we impose on it. Generations continue to be born, and we experience neither total apocalypse nor a happily-ever-after with any collective meaning beyond the endings of individual lives. Yet this narrative sense remains with us, flickering like a ghost through the revisions of postmodernism: we hope for resolution, or at least we hope that retrospectively what felt like a crisis will turn out to have been a turning point.

The novel—specifically, the European novel—was the grounds of Said's training as a reader and a scholar, and it was one of his long-standing intellectual passions. The novel was the principal lens through which he viewed the world, and it lay at the heart of many of the ideas and arguments that he has given to us. In North American popular discourse, Said may have been painted as a radical political figure, but he was first and foremost a literary scholar. The relationship between European traditions of representation, literary and otherwise, and the operations of imperial power was a relationship that he specifically trained our eyes upon. Still, the novel remained his subject, one that he loved. He held the complications of its heritage in his sight. He chose to read the so-called canon "contrapuntally"—a helpful Saidian term—rather than disavowing texts written in previous eras out of retrospective feelings of disgust, based on what he saw as their implication in systems of oppression and domination. Of course, later on, he himself saw this literary tradition less and less as a sole privilege of the West but rather as something shared by everyone, complexly; a tradition interpenetrated by cultures of the East and the South, and also inherited by them. In what often feels like a cynical age, I have found Said's engagement with fiction as an heir to a particular kind of humanism encouraging and even consoling: a humanism that can evolve and expand beyond its exclusionary, bourgeois European and largely male origins, and that commits itself to crossing boundaries between cultures and disciplines—a humanism that holds the practice of criticism close to heart.

Writing novels, in my experience, a writer has to at various points and to varying degrees sustain a split consciousness. On the one hand, we must admit that novels are a form of entertainment, existing somewhere between movies and poems. They are narrative objects made of language with, usually, a beginning, middle, and an end. They are a form that was born in the age of mechanical reproduction, and they are sold as commodities, an activity that today has rather a lot more to do with branding and marketing than it used to—a fact that is particularly confusing and troubling to exactly the type of person who might end up spending their time reading and writing novels. And on the other hand, there is a relationship between novels and what for want of a better phrase you might call our spiritual lives. Some of us read them for comfort, or to escape; some to learn about the world; some because it's a rare chance for concentrated solitude, to be neither working nor passively consuming the content of a screen but thinking deeply about experiences other than our own using some of the tools of our dream life, and listening carefully to the voices of others, in ways that ask for our imaginative participation and that might also shed light upon our own experiences of being alive on this planet. Novels reflect the perpetuation of a human impulse to use and experience narrative form as a way of making sense of the world. This may seem obvious. As a person who tries to spend most of her time reading and writing novels, I sometimes find that these two realities coexist without issue. But often I find myself distracted by and even anxious about the mystery of what these texts really do in the world, beyond providing mere escapism or misguided attempts at moral instruction, which I don't believe in either as a proper use of the form. Said tells us that "texts are worldly, to some degree they are events, and, even when they appear to deny it, they are nevertheless a part of the social world, human life, and of course the historical moments in which they are located and interpreted." This may be true, but it doesn't really help me, a writer, in thinking about what it is that I am doing when I sit down at my desk. Frank Kermode said that "fictions are for finding things out, and they change as the needs of sense-making change"— which I find a helpful formulation for thinking about how the novel, shape-shifting, strives for novelty, and how this relates to our need to find and create meaning. But most helpfully of all, for me, is what Sylvia Wynter said about the novel being a *revolutionary* form because it "is in essence a question mark." Perhaps a writer doesn't need to have a clear sense of what her text will do in the world. Perhaps a writer can relax a bit. Perhaps it's enough to ask a question, and hope, perhaps, to glimpse the meaning of that question in retrospect.

All writers have tics, a particular repertoire of moves that recur: mine is probably the construction of recognition scenes, or moments of what Aristotle in his *Poetics* called *anagnorisis*. Recognition scenes are not rare in fictional narrative; in fact, they are incredibly common. You'll notice them in popular novels with unreliable narrators or dramatic plot twists; in soap operas and in Hollywood films. Nor are they a feature of only the Western canon, either; they seem to be intrinsic to all storytelling traditions—as

Philip Kennedy, for instance, showed recently in his meticulous study of recognition scenes in the Arabic literary tradition, including in Quranic stories and the *Maqamat* of al-Hariri. Aristotle himself was analyzing plays that had been performed a hundred years beforehand, so he was noticing preexisting narrative paradigms and naming them, rather than inventing them. And he gave the word *anagnorisis* to the moment when the truth of a matter dawns on a character, that moment toward which a plot usually barrels, and around which a story's mysteries revolve. In the classic shape of rising action that reaches a peak before falling with the denouement or the unraveling, it's at the peak, at the moment of tragic reversal, that the anagnorisis usually takes place. In my case I think the persistence of this particular literary paradigm has to do in part with my feeling that fiction uniquely deals in subjectivities, in unstable narrative knowledge, in the limitations of perspective, and how different, limited perspectives interact. But I think it's also bound up with the fact that I have so far in my writing life been writing mostly about Palestine.

I will illustrate this with a story. There was once a king whose city was ravaged by a plague. This king heard two prophecies. The first declared that the plague was the result of regicide, the murder of the previous king, whose assassin was never caught. The second told him, cryptically, that he, the king himself, was the criminal he was seeking. Then the king's own wife, the queen, who had been previously married, recited a prophecy *she'd* once heard, which was that her first husband would be killed by his own son—this was a prophecy that did not, in fact, come true, since he was instead killed by a group of bandits at a fork in a road. Upon hearing this, our king is confused. He recalls yet another prophecy he heard long ago: that he would one day kill his father and marry his mother.

The king, of course, is Oedipus, the city is Thebes, the wife is Jocasta, and the murdered predecessor-king is Laius, who turns out to have been Oedipus's father. This ordering of events follows the play by Sophocles, which is estimated to have been first performed in the year 429 before the Common Era. Based on an already well-known myth, this play formed the substance of much of Aristotle's analysis of tragic drama in the *Poetics*, as well as, by now more famously, Sigmund Freud's theories of the family romance and the origins of civilization. For Freud, as for Aristotle, Greek tragedy held a special position in the Western cultural tradition, indicating where, in Freud's words, "religion, morals, society and art converge in the Oedipus complex."

I'm interested in the moment when a shepherd appears in the story. The shepherd is a witness, who comes bearing the truth to the king. The shepherd tells the king that a long time ago he handed a child over to a messenger, with orders to expose the baby on a mountainside, thus averting a prophecy that he would grow up to kill his father. The shepherd goes on to say that the messenger had disobeyed him and instead gave the baby to the queen of Corinth. This baby was the child of Laius. Oedipus is the criminal he seeks. The couple who raised him, the king and queen of Corinth, are not his real parents. Suddenly the multiple foregoing prophecies of the play reveal their interrelation; the truth pops out: Oedipus has *already* killed his father and married his mother. This is the moment of recognition.

Aristotle describes anagnorisis as a movement from ignorance to knowledge. When a character realizes the truth of a situation they are in, or the truth of their own identity or someone else's, the world of the text becomes momentarily intelligible to the protagonist and thus also to the audience. It's anagnorisis when

Darth Vader says to Luke Skywalker: "I am your father." It's anagnorisis when the coffin opens and Holly Martins sees the face not of Orson Welles but of another, third man. The mysteries clarify. Everything we thought we knew has been turned on its head, and yet it all makes sense.

Here's another one. After a war, which, lasting a mere six days, fails to regain territory lost twenty years earlier, and results instead in the loss of more territory to the enemy, a married couple, refugees for twenty years, take the opportunity offered by the disappeared border to visit the home they had lost by the coast. They drive north in an anxious silence. They are returning not victorious, as they had hoped, but on the wings of a defeat. And not only did they leave a house behind: through the force of tragic circumstance, they also left a baby, whom they were unable to go back for, faced with the flood of other refugees. Arriving now at the home not seen for twenty years, the couple sits with the woman who lives there. The woman quickly reveals that her son, who is about to arrive, is not hers biologically: she adopted him when she first arrived in the city, and moreover, he resembles the visiting couple. In other words, this is the same child they left in that original instance of flight. The woman's face turns yellow with dread. She says they must leave it up to him to choose his parentage. The son arrives wearing the uniform of the enemy army. Meeting his biological parents, he immediately denies them. He asserts that his only father died in Sinai eleven years before.

This is Ghassan Kanafani's novel *Returning to Haifa*, in which the characters Said and Safiyya return to the city—leaving their second son, Khalid, in Ramallah—to find their first child, Khaldun, has become Dov, adopted by a Jewish couple who are refugees from Europe and now live in their home. In this story, Dov denies the significance of parentage, of the bloodline. But then, seeming to contradict himself, Dov lashes out with reproach at Said and Safiyya: they should not have left him behind as a baby, he says; they should have fought with arms to retrieve him.

Like the Oedipus story, the plot here is based on a perverted family reunion. What is recognized, however, is not kinship, exactly: this is no recuperation of the stranger as the familiar, with all the potentially tragic fallout of that revelation, but rather, through the act of denial, a recognition that kinship is insufficient. Man is not just flesh and blood, says the protagonist, in a flash of insight: man is a cause. What this means is that it is not enough for the bonds of personal and political identity to be passively inherited but that they must be imprinted with intention and will. The scene has pivoted: the returning father sees how his fixation on the lost eldest child has obscured his view of the other, the second son in Ramallah, whom he forbade from joining the fida'iyeen. Counterpointed to his own pastward perspective, clinging to the ghosts of the Nakba, he perceives with sudden clarity that this younger son's desire to fight expresses a contrary, forward-looking gaze. Khalid looks to the Palestine of the future, not of the past. Thus the failed recognition of the eldest son leads to the proper recognition of the younger.

Of course, recognition is a figure of comedies as well, or stories with happy endings, often prompted by some physical sign that reveals who someone truly is. Like Odysseus, whose nurse knows him by his scar—or the comic tradition from Shakespeare all the way up to nineteenth-century comedies of manners like *The Importance of Being Earnest* and beyond, whose plots depend on mistaken identity, and whose climactic scenes untie jumbles of narrative threads and bring the stories to a conclusion. Recognition in these cases is quite literally the realization of *who someone is*: the person you thought was a stranger is actually a member of the family. There is an overfamiliar version of this—when a character removes their mask, when it turns out it was all a dream—when the paradigm feels formulaic or clichéd and fails to supply any real meaning. In *Returning to Haifa*, Kanafani gestures to this risk, in this translation by Karen E. Riley:

> Slowly the minutes passed, while everything remained motionless. Then the young man began to pace slowly: three steps toward the middle of the room, three steps toward the door, then back to the middle of the room. He set his cap on the table, and somehow it seemed inappropriate, almost laughable, next to the wooden vase full of peacock feathers. The strange sensation came over Said that he was watching a play prepared ahead of time in detail. It reminded him of cheap melodramas in trivial movies with artificial plots.

This gesture saves Kanafani's plot from succumbing to the jaded overfamiliarity of the classic recognition scene: by giving this thought to his protagonist, Kanafani preempts our doubt, acknowledging the history of the literary figure. A kind of prophylactic against readerly disbelief, it also paves the way for the switch, for the expected recognition scene to become nonrecognition, misfiring, failure.

Where the mood of the comic narrative is one of reunion and return—where resolution is total, the circle is closed—the novels I'm interested in may conclude, but they don't usually answer the questions they have posed. In tragedy, as in the novel, as in life, humanity's accounts with the forces of fate or circumstance or chance do not balance: what we might call the gods are willful, incomprehensible, and unfair. It's certainly not fair on poor old Oedipus: how was he supposed to know that Jocasta was his mother? At the same time, it's hard to consider the plot of Sophocles's *Oedipus the King* and not wonder why Oedipus did not at least put the pieces together before the shepherd got there with his eyewitness testimony. Both Terence Cave and Piero Boitani have pointed out that the Ancient Greek terms for recognition, reader, and reading—*anagnôrisis*, *anagnôstês*, and *anagnôsis*—are closely related both phonetically and conceptually. Oedipus seems to need a particular kind of "reliable" witness testimony as evidence in order to *read* the situation properly, in order to believe his eyes.

The novel *A Heart So White*, by the Spanish writer Javier Marías, begins with the words "I did not want to know but I have since come to know." Encased in this "I did not want to know" is an already-knowing. The reversal hastened by recognition functions only on account of an accumulation of knowledge, knowledge that has not been confronted. That's why it's re-cognition; ana-gnorisis: knowing again. In an interview, Marías said that while for some the novel "is a way of imparting knowledge," for him "it is more a way of imparting recognition of things that you didn't know you knew. You say 'yes.' It feels true even though it might be uncomfortable." To recognize something is, then, to perceive clearly what on some level you have known all along, but that perhaps you did not want to know.

Palestinians are familiar with such scenes in real life: apparent blindness followed by staggering realization. When someone, a stranger, suddenly comes to know what perhaps they did not want to know. A few months ago, I was in Palestine with a group of international writers for the Palestine Festival of Literature, a traveling festival with a strong pedagogical element: while the evenings are devoted to readings and panel discussions, the daytimes are jam-packed with tours and talks for the visiting writers. Several of these writers experienced something like tragic awakening. They said things like "My youth is gone" and "I have walked through a door and it has locked behind me." These were not even people who needed to be brought over from a distant political position: they came to Palestine with the desire to learn. They visited Hebron, and saw the soldiers patrolling, guarding settlers; they visited the destroyed town of al-Lydd; they navigated checkpoints; they traveled through Jerusalem and crossed in and out of the West Bank; they listened to statistics of killings and imprisonments and nighttime raids and asked careful questions. They seemed genuinely changed by the experience. I was moved to see them moved. At the same time, I couldn't help but feel a kind of despairing déjà vu, the scene of recognition having become at this point rather familiar.

We are at a moment when elementary democratic values the world over have eroded and in some places almost completely disappeared.

I feel it as a kind of fracturing of intention. The big emancipatory dreams of progressive and anticolonial movements of the previous century seem to be in pieces, and some are trying to make something with these pieces, taking language from here and from there to keep our movements going. The historically international significance of the Palestinian cause, first as a pan-Arab issue in the mid-twentieth century and later as an internationalist leftist one, has changed. Increased normalization with Israel by Arab states is a symptom of the ways Palestine has been abandoned in the region. The question of Palestine, couched often in the question of antisemitism, has torn up political debate in the UK, and while increasing numbers in the Democratic establishment in the United States openly express support and solidarity for the Palestinian cause and condemn the Israeli regime, speech in support of Palestinian rights is punished at the highest levels.

Until recently, Palestine had all but faded from diplomatic view under a quagmire of successive unsuccessful peace negotiations brokered by the United States, while right-wing and neoliberal forces pushed out the progressive left across the world—even as the question of Palestine continues to capture more of the mainstream of that left, even as more and more people cotton on to the realities of settler colonialism and ethnic cleansing, to the fact that Zionist ideology is ethnocentric and expansionist, and to the pernicious fiction that this is a fight between two equal sides. Individual moments of recognition are repeatedly overwhelmed by the energy of a political establishment that tells the onlooker: this is not what it looks like. It is too complicated to understand. Look away.

2022 was the deadliest year since 2005 for Palestinians in the West Bank. Since the start of 2023 Israeli forces have to date already killed 233 Palestinians and made 140 families homeless

(about 800 people), while settlers have conducted at least 315 attacks against Palestinians
and their property. There are 5200 Palestinians
in Israeli prisons, 1200 of whom are in administrative detention without charge, subjected
to torture and humiliation. Khader Adnan,
as one example, was arrested thirteen times
throughout his life, spent a total of eight years
in administrative detention, was never tried,
and died after his fifth hunger strike, which
lasted three months. We see so-called suicide
drones deployed on Palestinian populations in
Gaza. We witness helicopters dropping bombs
on West Bank towns, sights not seen in twenty
years. Pogroms conducted by settlers, protected
by soldiers. Open declarations of racism and
fascism by the Israeli government, while by no
means new, are becoming audible to Western
ears. The mask has truly been taken off.

I once heard Palestinian activist and co-founder
of the BDS movement, Omar Barghouti, talking

about an "aha moment"—what I would call, as you might by now have guessed, recognition. He was talking specifically about the moment when an Israeli realizes, in a turning point of action, that a Palestinian is a human being, just like him or her.

I have heard a few stories of such aha moments. One of them I was told about ten years ago by a young Israeli man whom I met by chance in the Galilee. I was on a trip to the Golan Heights with a Palestinian friend and an Israeli who, as his condition for driving us there, wanted to stop off at a kibbutz to convince a girl he had a crush on to come with us. We spent a few hours at this kibbutz in the Galilee, and tried, ultimately unsuccessfully, to persuade the young woman—and while we were sitting on the floor for a meal, a young, bearded man appeared in the doorway, introduced himself as Daniel, and sat down next to me. Something was up with Daniel. He was skittish. He kept asking me whether I thought we humans could ever act in the world purely as individuals, and not on behalf of groups. "For ourselves, alone," he kept saying, "and not for our groups." I didn't know what to tell him. Everyone else began pontificating about group-think, tribalism, Western individualism. Daniel rephrased the same question and asked it twice more. Then, eventually, he told me a story of deserting the army, and I understood from the story and from his manner that he was in hiding. He started by telling me, with a strange modesty, that he had been a "little" colonel, stationed at the Gaza fence, in charge of one other soldier. His instructions were the following: if anyone comes within a certain distance of the fence, you shoot once at the ground to warn them not to come closer. If they come closer but still within a certain distance, you shoot twice at the ground to warn them. And if they come closer than that, you shoot them in the leg. Daniel told me that he and his subordinate waited day after day at their station, and nobody came. And then, one day, a man appeared in the distance. He was walking toward them. He came within the first perimeter of the fence, and this little colonel shot once at the ground to warn him. The man came closer, so he shot twice at the ground to warn him. And as the man came closer again, Daniel could see that he was entirely naked. And that he was holding something out before him. And as he came still closer, Daniel could see he was holding a photograph, and that it was a photograph of a child. He did not shoot the man in the leg. He put down his gun and fled.

How many Palestinians, asked Omar Barghouti, need to die for one soldier to have their epiphany?

Many Palestinians have nevertheless devoted their lives and careers to actively trying to induce epiphanies in other people. The people they are trying to persuade, however, are not usually Israeli soldiers. Unless they are among the very small minority who "break the silence" through available domestic channels that sometimes challenge state propaganda and Zionist supremacist ideology, soldiers simply reproduce state propaganda and ideology. Indeed, they are a key feature of both. The idea that Jewish Israelis at large might be persuaded through dialogue to see Palestinians as human is also absurd, given that Israelis live in a militarized society in which dissent is punished. The destined audience of this persuasion is rather the unaffiliated onlooker, the foreigner, the one who has not yet reckoned with how much they are already, if unwittingly—historically, politically, economically—involved in the lives of others.

Destined to be the victims of the victims, swamped by a Western master-narrative of Jewish redemption, the story of the Palestinians has struggled to reach audiences in the global north, as Said decried in his famously titled 1984 essay, "Permission to Narrate": "Facts do not at all speak for themselves, but require a socially acceptable narrative to absorb, sustain and circulate them. Such a narrative has to have a beginning and end: in the Palestinian case, a homeland for the resolution of its exile since 1948. [. . .] [The] acceptance of a narrative entailing a homeland [. . .] has been resisted as strenuously on the imaginative and ideological level as it has been politically."

But the story of the Palestinian struggle has always been an international one, even when the existence of Palestinians as a people was denied, or verbally replaced with the euphemistic label "non-Jews," which first officially appeared in the 1917 Balfour Declaration declaring British support for the establishment of a Jewish homeland in Palestine. The Israeli state as a Jewish democracy to which Palestinian Arabs have always posed a demographic threat was a state born from European empire, cast in the mold of other European settler colonial projects, and it was both fueled and justified by a history of European racism and antisemitism. The future of the Palestine question is bound up with the domestic politics and histories of a handful of countries: mostly the United States, the United Kingdom, France, and Germany. Once Palestinian voices began to reach wider audiences in the West, the story was quickly cast as a war of two opposing narratives, rather than a holistic and variegated history of European racism and empire and the ensuing and ongoing history of American empire, and the concomitant struggles for self-determination by colonized peoples, from Haiti to Algeria to Vietnam.

Aristotle says that tragedy compresses time: in real life we do not usually have sudden moments of recognition; normally we learn and grow and change gradually, if indeed we change at all. But I'm perhaps unusually familiar with the extremely dramatic nature of revelations in real life because I have seen it and heard about it happening so many times. And I suppose I retain a kind of faith in at least the possibility of a swift movement from ignorance to knowledge, as a kind of human possibility, even as my faith in its political possibilities has become increasingly cautious as time goes on. We are in new territory now. The Palestinian struggle for freedom has outlasted the narrative shape of other anticolonial liberation movements that concluded with independence during the twentieth century, and it is becoming more difficult to hold fast to the old narratives about the power of narrative.

When I was in graduate school, I tried to write a short story inspired by this meeting with the soldier. The story followed a Palestinian and an Israeli going to visit the Golan Heights together. The Palestinian is a West Bank resident, and his permit to be inside the 1948 territories will expire at midnight. A snowstorm interrupts their journey, and the Israeli, who is upset about a girl they meet en route, leaves the Palestinian to return to the West Bank alone, without a car. On their journey, the story is full of people telling one another stories about their moments of recognition. I submitted the story for workshop, and my teacher's response was: "This piece is highly recursive. There are things I admired, but it is fundamentally a depressed story. Every time someone tells a story you undermine the climax." He also pointed to the appearance of a large black dog at the kibbutz shaking snow off its fur, which makes a little girl scream. He wrote in the margin, "This is you!" I didn't mean to include the black dog as a symbol of depression. I wanted to respond, "But it's an image I included randomly, something I saw in life! It just stuck in my mind, this big dog I saw shaking its fur and a little girl screaming in surprise!" But I didn't, of course, because that is one of the weakest defenses in a creative writing workshop—to protest, when something doesn't work aesthetically, by saying: But it really happened! And also because I knew that writers are not always in conscious control of their work and that I could not in good faith tell my teacher that he was wrong.

Maybe the failure of this story was a sign not only of my pessimism and grief about the political context but also of how I was struggling with the staleness of the paradigm—and maybe these two things are connected. I was still working out how to write an effective, authentic recognition scene. The Palestinian struggle has gone on so long now that it is easy to feel disillusioned with the scene of recognition as a site of radical change, or indeed as a turning point at all.

It's here that I want to bring in the idea of the epiphany, a word I've already used, and a concept which, by virtue of the suddenness of its process and its relationship to knowledge, is close to recognition. In layman's terms, an epiphany is a eureka moment. But in literary art, we associate epiphany primarily with the short story form rather than with the novel, and most particularly with James Joyce. In Joyce's stories, the epiphanic moment is not usually a moment of understanding, however, but one that introduces a shift of perspective. A kind of partial turn. It's more often a disclosure that knowledge itself is precarious. Some meaning may arise, precipitating the ending, but it does not mean closure. The word *epiphany* itself comes from the Koine Greek word ἐπιφάνεια, *epipháneia*, meaning manifestation or appearance, derived from the verb φαίνειν, *phainein*, meaning to appear. It is usually applied in Ancient Greek contexts to three things: the first is dawn, the second is the appearance of an enemy army, and the third is the manifestation of a deity. The third one is obviously what led to its use in the Bible and subsequently provided the meaning that the Catholic-born James Joyce subverted, detheologizing it in his writing. But it's the first two—dawn, and the appearance of the enemy army—that are interesting to me, because they suggest something appearing beyond the horizon, beyond the field of vision that your subject position allows, with the revelation of threat and light.

I suspect that if I'd had this in my mind at the time, my story might have been a bit more successful.

A problem with Barghouti's example of an Israeli soldier's epiphany and my own is that they center the non-Palestinian as the one who experiences the decentering shock of recognizing Palestinian humanity. It was, after all, on the little colonel's horizon that that man in Gaza appeared, walking toward him without his clothes on, literally risking his life to undertake this desperate performance of his humanity, saying, *look at me naked, I am a human being,* holding up a photograph of a child, who we easily imagine was his own child, killed by Israeli missile fire. There's another version of this same story that does not involve anagnorisis but is instead a familiar repeating tragedy of living in a constant state of fear of having your home destroyed, of losing loved ones or your own life to bombs dropped from the sky from which there is no shelter. And yet the pressure is again on Palestinians to tell the human story that will educate and enlighten others and so allow for the conversion of the repentant Westerner, who might then descend onto the stage if not as a hero then perhaps as some kind of deus ex machina. It is easy to be caught between desperately wanting to convince people and feeling fed up at how slow they are to understand, bitter at their high emotional tenor when they finally experience their epiphanies and issue their apartheid reports, and still incredibly grateful that their recognition has given rise to concrete action.

I do think that there is another way we can frame this, one which focuses less on who is the main character or who is the victim, which I draw from Yasmin El-Rifae's brilliant book *Radius*, about a militant feminist group protecting women from sexual assault in Tahrir Square toward the end of the 2011 Egyptian revolution. El-Rifae ponders the analogous issue of women appealing to or trying to educate men about misogyny and patriarchal violence. "Rather than wondering about the efficacy of addressing men," she asks, "can we think of breaking into their awareness as a by-product of us speaking to one another? Can we focus instead on our own networks, on thinking together, on resisting together, on supporting one another— openly?" Writing in English about Palestine, I often find myself asked if my aim is to educate "Westerners," a suggestion I always find reductive and kind of undignified. But I like this idea of breaking into the awareness of other people by talking candidly among ourselves.

If there was another lesson I learned here, in the episode of writing my depressed story, it was the quite basic one that literature is not life, and that the material we draw from the world needs to undergo some metamorphosis in order to function, or even to live, on the page.

* * *

Many first novels are disguised autobiographies; mine was a disguised biography, although I didn't bother to disguise it very well. The novel followed the life of my great-grandfather, Midhat Kamal, who was born in the town of Nablus when Palestine was part of Greater Syria under the Ottoman Empire. Midhat went to study in the south of France as a young man, and returned to Nablus as British Mandate rule commenced.

Throughout my childhood, which I spent in London, this picture was on our kitchen cupboard. It's a photo that has been replicated many times among my extended family. Everyone seems to have a photograph of a photograph of it in their living room. I have never seen the original.

My dad and his siblings always spoke lovingly of Midhat: he was a kind, gentle, and quite hilarious man, known locally as "the Parisian" or "Al-Barisi" for his love of all things French. Midhat did not go to the bank, he went to the *banque*; his socks always matched his *mouchoir*; and after bathing he used to ask my aunt to slap his *colognia* on his back—and while such affectations might be fairly common among the wealthy Lebanese, especially after Lebanon became a French protectorate, this was not very common in Nablus. What I was told about Midhat's Francophilia and his love affairs sat at variance with another, more common narrative that all kids in the diaspora grow up with: the narrative of displacement, war, oppression. My picture of him was drawn from this photograph: a man out for a walk in Paris, perhaps in the Bois de Boulogne, holding a pair of gloves, looking chic and pleased with himself. A year after leaving university, I decided I wanted to write a novel based on Midhat's life. In part, I wanted to tell a story about Palestinian lives before the foundation of Israel. But I was mostly motivated by my own curiosity about life there during that period, as well as, more specifically, my curiosity about Midhat himself.

There are many obstacles to writing well about Palestine before the Nakba. The main one is nostalgia. Personal memory is already notoriously unreliable, and nostalgia, when it afflicts an entire people, can have an even more corrosive effect on memory. Nostalgia makes us generalize and forget the particular. When you speak to refugees about Palestine, they will often describe the fig trees, the olive trees, the lost heaven of their childhoods. Over the course of the first year I spent interviewing elderly people about their memories, I began to wonder whether it was easier to divert to these general images, which everyone had access to, than to recall the particular rooms, the particular objects, the particular people they had lost.

In the end, I took this to mean I had creative license in those places where memory fogged, or where I couldn't find written records, or when personal testimonies contradicted each other. I'm going to give an example that is a spoiler, so if you haven't read my first book and plan to, try to forget it afterward. Midhat, late in the novel, experiences a kind of psychotic break and spends some time in a mental institution. This is true. The facts I meddled with were the following: in real life, the hospital was not in Bethlehem but in Cairo. In real life, he "broke down" when he found out he had been disinherited by his father; I changed this so that the betrayal is felt through discovering a letter from his French girlfriend, which his father had hidden from him—a letter that retrospectively changes Midhat's understanding of what had happened in France. Both the disinheritance and the hiding of the letter are based on genuine betrayals by his father, but I reorganized the facts around the second deceit. This was *not factually accurate*, but it got to what I perceived to be the truth of the matter. That a young man's hopes for the future were repeatedly, devastatingly shot down, and not just by circumstance but by his own father—whose actions are experienced by the child as an abandonment on the level of that suffered by Oedipus at the hands of his parents, or of Khaldun's by his—this was an essential wound that, once recognized, ruptures all harmony between the mind and the social world (or exposes their disjunction) and forces a reevaluation of both past and present reality.

In other words, it was the revealing fiction. It allowed me to create my own moment of anagnorisis—centered, naturally, on the act of reading; in this case, reading a letter.

It's strange because I grew up with this photograph, but only many years later, once I was partway through writing my first book, did I actually look at it properly. I find this hard to believe about myself, that I could be so unperceptive, but it confirms the fact that received ideas or ideas from childhood can be hard to untie, even when faced with the evidence of your senses. I suddenly realized that Midhat is not outdoors, walking in the Bois du Boulogne. He is standing in front of a painted screen. The photograph was taken in a photography studio in Jerusalem in 1923.

What I learned through writing this book is that literary anagnorisis feels most truthful when it is not redemptive: when it instead stages a troubling encounter with limitation or wrongness. This is the most I think we can hope for from novels: not revelation, not the dawning of knowledge, but the exposure of its limit. To realize you have been wrong about something is, I believe, to experience the otherness of the world coming at you. It is to be thrown off-center. When this is done well in literature, the readerly experience is deeply pleasurable. Terence Cave argues in his book on the subject that it is the reader herself who craves the tragic reversal, because fictions have a capacity "to astonish us, upset us, change our perceptions in ways inaccessible to other uses of language."

To give some examples from contemporary fiction, we can look at the novels of Deborah Levy—*The Man Who Saw Everything*, or her latest, *August Blue*, or *Swimming Home*. There's often a moment, pivoting on the hinge of a repeated word or image, when things click into place, the lock turns, the trail of strange symbols suddenly reveal their meaningful interrelation, and the stage machinery rotates. We understand what the horse is, the meaning of the jaguar, the bear, the gun under the bed—sometimes it's the meaning of the title that is revealed. As in Elena Ferrante's Neapolitan Quartet, when we realize that the brilliant friend of the first book's title is not Lila, it's our narrator, Lenù—the only times the phrase appears in the text are in reference to Lenù in Lila's conception—one of many instances in which we feel the hard edge of Lenù's knowledge. There is an intensity of pleasure when we glimpse a character's limit in this way, when a sense of the real, of that which is contrary, opaque, other, pokes through the gaps of their and our perception. The author gives us the feeling of confronting the wall of our under-standing, the exhilarating feeling of being wrong.

Anne Carson, in her essay "'Just for the Thrill': Sycophantizing Aristotle's 'Poetics,'" also confronts the quandary of understanding this pleasure. She writes:

> But the question of what exactly it is we enjoy in the experience of recognizing our own error, at that moment when the soul turns to look at its own reasoning process like an actor upon a stage and intervenes just in time to forestall kidnap, seems to be a question fundamental to our understanding of Aristotle's understanding of what poetry is. "No brush can write two words at the same time," says the classical Chinese proverb. Yet Aristotelian mimesis is just such a brush, able to paint knowledge and error shaking hands with one another in a mirror.

There's much to say about the images that Carson conjures here: the staging of the errors of the soul as a play, recognition as forestalling a theatrical act of violence—a kidnap—and an act of witnessing that takes place both inside and outside the text simultaneously. Somehow error and knowledge shake hands *in the mirror* and also, in an impossible image, through it.

What in fiction is enjoyable and beautiful is often terrifying in real life. In real life, shifts in collective understanding are necessary for major changes to occur, but on the human, individual scale, they are humbling and existentially disturbing. Such shifts also do not usually come without a fight: not everyone can be unpersuaded of their worldview through argument and appeal, or through narrative. Maggie Nelson, in *The Art of Cruelty*, punctures the high-minded moralism of art that seeks, through depicting suffering, to move an audience to do something about it. "Having a strong reaction is not the same thing as having an understanding," she writes, "and neither is the same thing as taking an action." It's true that emotion and understanding are not the same as action, but you might say that understanding is necessary for someone to act.

Of course, the word *recognition* has another, very formal connotation in political discourse as a diplomatic or governmental action; states will recognize the sovereignty of another state or political entity, or a political or legal claim, or a right to life, a right to have rights. Cultural recognition of difference can form the basis of just societies, but recognition that remains *solely* that—a form of acknowledgment without economic and political redistribution—is an act of language that leaves out the plot of history, where a word tries to stand in for material reparations through the smoke and mirrors of discourse and ceremony. The recognition of Indigenous peoples by settler colonial societies, including acknowledging First Nation territories, might be a place to start, but it is no place to end. In the Palestinian case, the Oslo

Accords of the nineties, which inaugurated a misleadingly titled "peace process" and led to an entrenchment of Israeli occupation, prominently featured letters of mutual recognition between the PLO and Israel. The PLO was recognized as the legitimate representative of the Palestinian people: granted the mantle of statecraft without an actual state.

In the language of both law and literary form, then, recognition is a kind of knowing that *should incur* the responsibility to act for it to have any value beyond personal epiphanies, or appeasing the critics of the one doing the recognizing. Great effort is required to ensure that such a moment marks the middle of the story, and not the finale. Another act must follow.

The fact is, huge edifices do move in human history. Empires have fallen. The Berlin Wall fell, political apartheid in South Africa did end, and although in neither of these cases were these putative conclusions by any means the end of the story, they are testaments to the fact that, under the force of coordinated international and local action, Israeli apartheid will also end. The question is, when and how? Where in the narrative do we now stand?

Facing the antagonists of misinformation, widespread censorship, and a military superpower backed by the United States—which has to date provided Israel with more than $260 billion adjusted for inflation in bilateral (largely military) assistance and missile defense funding—and that trains its weapons upon the stateless Palestinian population, feels like trying to scale an incredibly large wall with your bare hands. How to confront this except perhaps with what the Palestinian novelist Emile Habibi named "pessoptimism"—an acutely Palestinian frame of mind? Gramsci, borrowing from Romain Rolland, described this condition only slightly less concisely as "pessimism of the intellect, optimism of the will." It's one thing to see shifts on an individual level, but quite another to see them on an institutional or governmental one. To induce a person's change of heart is different from challenging the tremendous force of collective denial.

And denial is arguably the opposite of recognition. But even denial is based on a kind of knowing. A willful turning from devastating knowledge, perhaps, out of fear. Think of Khaldun/Dov, denying his parents who have finally returned to Haifa. Of Peter denying Christ three times. Think of climate change denial. Think of the slave traders and economists of the nineteenth century who claimed that ending the enslavement of human beings was economically and politically unviable. The strength of their stated convictions resembles the arguments of the gun lobby in the US today, and of governments regarding the use of fossil fuels, and arguments that sanctioning occupying powers on the basis of crimes they commit against humanity is impossible. We've seen evidence very recently that this is not impossible. In today's crisis of climate destruction, there will be moments—maybe they are happening right now, maybe they happened recently—that will later be narrated as turning points, when the devastating knowledge hits home to a greater and greater number that we are treating the earth as a slave, and that this exploitation is profoundly unethical. We are still seeking a language for this ethics.

Having thought through the paradigm of the recognition scene in this way, its limits and its uses, I want to make a partial turn as I end, to discuss, briefly, Said's 2003 lecture on Freud, "Freud and the Non-European," which became his final book. In this lecture, Said focuses on a particular manifestation of Freud's contribution to our understanding of the human mind—which, to speak very generally, was to decenter the conscious will by excavating that which we do not understand in our own selves. Acknowledging the alterity in our minds and hearts is to reconcile ourselves to ambivalence, strangeness, and internal disunity. In a way, you might say Freud converted those willful crazy Greek gods into the superego. The otherness that comes at you from the world has been inside you all along.

Freud's late work *Moses and Monotheism* posits that Moses, the Hebrew prophet, was actually Egyptian, and that "his ideas about a single God are derived entirely from the Egyptian Pharaoh," Said explains. For Said, this signals Freud's prevailing Eurocentrism giving way to a model of otherness at the root of Jewishness. He suggests that the work expresses, perhaps even *unconsciously*, Freud's reaction to Zionism and his refusal to submit to the ethnonationalism of Zionist ideology. This secret Egyptianness at the root of the Jewish religion, he argues, has been collectively repressed in the establishment of the Israeli state as an essentially European project in the Middle East. Freud's is a search for origins that destabilizes, he argues, an alternative archaeology to the Zionist archaeology that is used to legitimize the state-building project. Through looking at this late work of Freud's, Said dismantles the binaries he was occasionally accused of reifying, pointing to the position of a non-European non-Jew—"the great stranger"—at the heart of the Jewish story.

Crucially, in the light of this, he describes a non-Zionist model of being Jewish that has an "irremediably diasporic, unhoused character." He adds that "this needn't be seen only as a Jewish characteristic; in our age of vast population transfers, of refugees, exiles, expatriates and immigrants, it can also be identified in the diasporic, wandering, unresolved, cosmopolitan consciousness of someone who is both inside and outside his or her community." Said seems here, you might say, to be describing himself.

Thus Said reverses the scene of recognition as I have described it. Rather than recognizing the stranger as familiar, and bringing a story to its close, Said asks us to recognize the familiar as stranger. He gestures at a way to dismantle the consoling fictions of fixed identity, which make it easier to herd into groups. This might be easier said than done, but it's provocative—it points out how many narratives of self, when applied to a nation-state, might one day harden into self-centered intolerance. Narrative shape can comfort and guide our efforts, but we must eventually be ready to shape-shift, to be decentered, when the light of an other appears on the horizon in the project of human freedom, which remains undone.

Perhaps this is also a long, convoluted response to Daniel the soldier's question, which I never answered, about whether we can think for ourselves and not only on behalf of our groups. Perhaps by now he has read some Edward Said. Palestinianism was for Said a condition of chronic exile, exile as agony but also as ethical position. To remain aloof from the group while honoring one's organic ties to it; to exist between loneliness and alignment, remaining always a bit of a stranger; to resist the resolution of the narrative, the closing of the circle; to keep looking, to not feel too at home.

Afterword: On Gaza

Someone once told me she had interviewed an elderly Palestinian woman during the second intifada as part of an oral history project about Palestinians in the diaspora. This particular woman, she said, pointed at another woman wailing in distress on the television screen in her living room in London and cried: "That's me! That's me!" I found this story quite moving. Then I was told the woman's name, and learned that it was my own grandmother. I suddenly laughed, because my grandmother is very dramatic. Reflecting on this now, however, I find myself moved once more. What a pure relation, to see herself in the woman on the television, to experience the distance between them not as numbing but as another component of her pain. The present onslaught leaves no space for mourning, since mourning requires an afterward, but only for repeated shock and the ebb and flow of grief. We who are not there, witnessing from afar, in what ways are we mutilating ourselves when we dissociate to cope? To remain human at this juncture is to remain in agony. Let us remain there: it is the more honest place from which to speak.

When I delivered this Said Memorial Lecture in September 2023 it spoke of the long-standing reality of Palestinian subjugation to conditions of military occupation, settler colonialism, and apartheid, mostly incrementally but sometimes dramatically worsening, including recent increased settler violence, rapidly expanding settlements in the West Bank, and general impunity by the occupying power in their treatment of Palestinians with the full blessing of the United States. Nine days after I delivered it, the Qassam Brigades—the military wing of Hamas, the political movement in power in the Gaza Strip—launched a surprise attack by land, sea, and air on the Israeli military bases and kibbutzim in the Gaza envelope close to the partition fence, as well as a nearby rave. 1,139 Israelis were killed, including 695 civilians, by a mixture of Palestinian and some Israeli fire. Hamas militants abducted more than two hundred Israelis and announced that the ransom was the release of the five thousand Palestinian political prisoners who were then held in Israeli prisons. This guerilla operation, which must have been planned for years in secret, resembled an incredibly violent jailbreak. It also signified a paradigm shift: it showed that a system in which one population is afforded rights that the other population is denied will be safe for neither.

I'm sure that Israeli troops are indeed trying to root out Hamas fighters, and that, failing to achieve this, they instead show images of undressed Palestinian men and boys kneeling in rows for the purpose of raising domestic morale and concealing the shame of their military losses. Such facts do not contradict the genocidal rhetoric and practice of the state—over twenty-five thousand Palestinians in Gaza reported killed at the time I write this in January 2024, with more than eight thousand unaccounted for. The argument that Israel is exercising self-defense— already egregious when using military power against a population it occupies—in response to the Qassam Brigades operation of October 7 is untenable in the face of the wholesale slaughter, destruction of civilian infrastructure, and open discussion of mass transfer. Ten thousand dead children is not self-defense.

When the Egyptian writer and current political prisoner Alaa Abdel Fattah visited Gaza in 2012, he described the situation there as "like it's been sent back in time from some grim future we haven't arrived at yet" but to which all of us are headed. The first two months of this most recent Israeli assault saw at least 281,000 metric tons of carbon dioxide released into the atmosphere—greater than the annual carbon footprint of more than twenty of the world's most climate-vulnerable nations. How can we expect to care for our planet and its resources and our collective future if such atrocities can happen before our eyes with the support of the world's great powers? This attack is a cataclysm not only for Palestinians but for everyone.

I'm confident that these recent months have led to private moments of reckoning for many. The world has tolerated violence against Palestinians for a long time, but this attack has exceeded that violence to an extent that has at moments been intolerable even for those who consider themselves total bystanders. But while the world's majority may say no—hundreds of thousands in the streets of Algiers, Jakarta, London, even Berlin—US support for the Israeli government and its actions is as strong as ever. President Biden bypassed Congress to pledge an extra $14.3 billion in military aid in addition to the annual donation of $3.8 billion, and in the UN General Assembly vote on the resolution reaffirming the Palestinian right to self-determination, the US, broker of the so-called peace negotiations between Israel and the Palestinians, voted against it, just as they had voted against a humanitarian truce. Most crucially and shamefully, the US vetoed the Security Council resolution demanding an immediate humanitarian ceasefire on December 8, 2023. The image of US representative Robert Wood alone raising his hand in dissent should leave a stain on Western consciousness. At the time, eighteen thousand Palestinians in Gaza had already been killed by Israeli bombardment. In the US Congress a war of discourse mistranslates Arabic words like "intifada" as "genocide"; elsewhere, an occupied population is attacked in what many Holocaust and genocide experts have called either "a textbook case of genocide" or "a genocide in the making." The United States is acquainted with the crime, having facilitated genocides in other countries such as Indonesia and Guatemala, for which they never faced retribution; indeed Raphael Lemkin, who coined the term "genocide," considered the colonial replacement of Indigenous peoples by European colonists in the Americas to be a historical example of the crime. South Africa has now launched a case against Israel for committing genocide at the International Court of Justice; at the time I write, the court has found plausible grounds for the accusation and ordered interim measures to protect Palestinians in Gaza while they make their final determination, although they stopped short of calling for an immediate and permanent ceasefire. Israeli Prime Minister Benjamin Netanyahu has said in response to the proceedings at the Hague: "Nobody will stop us."

Ask the questions. Why should anybody have the power of veto in the UN Security Council? Why do Americans pay billions of tax dollars annually to a foreign war machine, deployed on a captive civilian population? If the United States and the United Kingdom both voted against the Palestinian right to self-determination should we interpret this to mean that the most powerful nations in the Anglosphere if not the Global North at large believe that Palestinians must remain a colonized and dispersed people forever? That Palestine must never be free, but must remain subject to Israeli apartheid from the Jordan River to the Mediterranean Sea? That Palestinians must remain subjected to daily violence, impoverishment in refugee camps, and permanent political alienation? The powers and principles that govern the world, hardly in hiding, reveal themselves now in three dimensions and technicolor.

"What would Edward Said say?" sounds like something you might find printed on a T-shirt, but I have recently been wondering what he would have said about this tremendous violence, and the abuse of the idea of antisemitism in the West to stifle speech in support of Palestinian rights in the face of what is clearly a long-standing project of ethnic cleansing. As a figure who worked in the heart of the Western academy, whose university, Columbia, is one of the major sites of this war of language—what would he say? When people are threatened and lose their jobs for speaking out against mass murder, and some have even faced arrest? What would he say about a world where it is controversial in Western democracies to call for a ceasefire?

In some sense, these attacks on speech are merely a continuation of the same aggression and attempts at silencing that Said himself faced. The FBI kept a file on him that was, at the time of his death, 238 pages long. He was a frequent recipient of hate mail and death threats. His office at Columbia was set on fire, the door was bashed with a baseball bat, and he was the only person in the university besides the president who had bulletproof windows and a panic button by his desk. Among Palestinians, Said is perceived as a moderate, but for the West he was dangerous: a person who did not mince his words, who did not cow to pieties. Were he alive today I don't doubt he would be speaking very clearly, raging at the punishment of students on his own campus, at the doublespeak of the establishment and of the most widely read newspapers and news channels in the US (and the UK) and their blatant double standards, at the co-opting of grief as a justification for assassinations and mass murder.

The war over words originates in the West's familiarity with the fact that hate speech is the first seemingly innocuous step on the road to genocide. But the West is stuck in a loop, always looking at the past (displaced into language), instead of at the present (communicated in images), from which they want to look away. The Eurocentrism of the definition may now be on trial at the Hague, but in dominant Western discourse, genocide can only be committed against the Jews because it once was, and therefore they are the only group that must be protected. While historians have classified massacres of Indigenous Americans and the Herero people as genocides, for example, no similar institutions or legal frameworks or systems of retribution have been constructed in their wake. Meanwhile, the memory of the Holocaust is starting to function like the murder of another famous Jew, who was also a Palestinian, and who was called Jesus Christ, and in whose name all manner of catastrophes have been perpetrated over the centuries, exploitations and violent nationalisms, crusades and manifest destinies.

It is a novel horror in human history to watch a genocidal war on our phones. For men, women, and children, scholars, artists, and journalists to live-tweet the moments before they are killed. Children blue with dust, tear tracks down their faces, look at us from our screens. Children blue with death. Unburied corpses lie strewn across the streets. A little girl, rescued from the rubble of her destroyed home and carried out on a stretcher by three men, asks if they are taking her to the cemetery. One of the men laughs in surprise, and tells her how beautiful she is, and that she is alive. But it is terrible: the girl has been preparing herself to die and now thinks she is dead. Israeli soldiers murder a pregnant woman holding a white flag. They murder three Israeli hostages who hold a white flag. A man who has lost his wife and children in an air strike clings to a shaft of rubble and screams from the bottom of his lungs: "Who do I hug? Tell me who do I hug?" A reporter, learning of the murder of his colleague, rips off his PRESS vest and helmet and says, "What is the point?" The journalist in the studio to whom he is speaking covers her face and weeps. The corpse of a child hangs from a building. Entire families have been wiped out. Cemeteries destroyed, bodies dug up, acronyms devised like "WCNSF": Wounded Child No Surviving Family. I am not the first to think of Picasso's *Guernica* when I see these images of wreckage, although I wonder if this is just another evasion. In 1982, the French writer Jean Genet recorded his impressions of Shatila refugee camp in Lebanon, a week after the massacre of Palestinians and Lebanese Shiites carried out by Phalangist forces with the support and help of the Israelis. "Photography is unable to capture the flies," he writes, "or the thick white smell of death. Nor can it tell about the little hops you have to make when walking from one corpse to the next." Watching through screens, I try to imagine what the phone camera and news channel images cannot catch, but sometimes, I confess, I find it so hard to see the corpses and the children with destroyed faces that I only look for a few seconds and then I can't look any longer.

A past has been demolished—universities, places of worship, writers, educators, journalists, little children, elderly people who remember the Nakba of 1948—and a future has been demolished. *What future?* you might ask. These people lived in a so-called open-air prison, under siege for seventeen years, their calorie-intake counted by the Israeli state, their living conditions already "uninhabitable." Yet there was a future there and it has been destroyed. Two million Palestinians have been displaced and their mass murder is live-streamed. Those in Gaza who do not die from the bombs die of starvation, or thirst, or infectious diseases, or the cold. Hundreds more have been killed and tens of thousands subjected to settler and military terror in the West Bank, and the number of Palestinians in Israeli military prisons has doubled. It is simultaneously true that the Nakba of 1948 never really ended and that we are currently watching it being repeated. An Israeli commander described the war on Gaza as "Nakba 2.0." As I write this, a ceasefire has still not been called. I wonder what reality you now live in. From the point in time at which you read this, what do you say of the moment I am in? How large is the gulf between us?

I can only write from my present moment, and speak from my limited viewpoint, conscious of the edges, even if I cannot always see them. It remains important to reach back in history for analogy, even though we might be punished for doing so, in order to frame and make sense of what is happening, to look at the Warsaw Ghetto, at the 1982 Israeli invasion of Beirut, the Tet Offensive in Vietnam, and to analogize and compare, to make use of universal concepts—and it is equally important to take stock of the particularities of the moment, and to recognize that we are hurtling somewhere new.

I began the lecture claiming that we can only identify turning points in retrospect. Given the speed and violence with which the cogs are presently rotating, it does feel like we might be in a turning point now: still, we don't know in which direction we are moving. Are we seeing the beginnings of a decolonial future, or of a more complete obliteration than the Nakba of 1948? The possibilities faced by the Israeli state for at least twenty years have been: maintain apartheid and forfeit the claim to being a democracy; return to the pre-1967 state borders and allow for the creation of a Palestinian state; break down the system of apartheid and enfranchise the Palestinians in a one-state reality; or conduct a large-scale ethnic cleansing. They are choosing the last option. Will the rest of the world let them get away with it? Or has Gaza now triggered a change in our world order, as people living in supposed democracies reckon with the exception of Palestine? Or is this the beginning of a capitulation to disintegrating consensus, and to the flimsiness of basic democratic principles and international law? Somewhere recently humanity seems to have crossed an invisible line, and on this side naked power combined with the will to profit threaten to overwhelm the collective interests of our species.

I also began with Said's idea of humanism, one that expands beyond the term's discriminatory origins which described humanness only in relation to the nonhumanness of Europe's various others. The mainstream Western media, in step with Israeli state rhetoric, has offered an abundance of proof that this colonial principle of selective humanity has never gone away. The Israeli minister of agriculture, Avi Dichter, as he justified bombing the strip, described the people of Gaza as "human animals"; National Security Minister Itamar Ben-Gvir has long used similar language to justify the oppression, collective punishment, and killing of Palestinians, as many Israeli leaders have before him. International law—the law and language of human rights—has never been applied equally. The rhetorical dehumanization of Palestinians since the beginning of the Zionist movement in the nineteenth century, entering the North American mainstream in the sixties, has long nurtured Israeli—and Western—public consent for the Zionist project.

In *Exterminate All the Brutes*, his 1996 study of the history of colonialism and genocides—title taken from Joseph Conrad's *Heart of Darkness*—Sven Lindqvist writes: "The idea of extermination lies no farther from the heart of humanism than Buchenwald lies from the Goethehaus in Weimar. That insight has been almost completely repressed, even by the Germans, who have been made sole scapegoats for ideas of extermination that are actually a common European heritage." This proximity of humanism—its institutions, its material effects—to coloniality and colonial violence remains as it was when Lindqvist wrote this, and not only in Europe. We see clearly what we are up against. Others understood this better and faster than I did, so this may be my own personal moment of recognition. To face a reality that on some level I knew all along, but that I did not want to know.

There is a temptation to leap forward rhetorically to reflect on the present: what will you have done? What that means is: there is still time. What that means is: time is running out. Every ten minutes, according to the WHO, a child is killed. It will be easy to say, in hindsight, what a terrible thing. That was a terrible moment, when the movements of the world were out of my hands.

Do not give in. Be like the Palestinians in Gaza. Look them in the face. Say: that's me! Mahmoud Darwish tells us: "Gaza does not propel people to cool contemplation; rather she propels them to erupt and collide with the truth." The Israeli government would like to destroy Palestine, but they are mistaken if they think this is really possible. Palestine is in Haifa. Palestine is in Jerusalem. Palestine is in Gaza and Palestine is in the Mediterranean Sea and Palestine is alive in the refugee camps, from Shatila to Yarmouk. Palestine is even alive and well in New York. Do they really believe they can obliterate the Palestinian will to life? Their seventy-six-year attempt—sometimes protracted, sometimes fast—to eliminate the native seems at times like the strategy of fools. Of course they will harden Gaza each time they bomb her; of course they will force her resistance fighters underground. Possibly they know this very well, and even desire it, since it provides a pretext to keep bombing. But they can never complete the process, because they cannot kill us all.

In his essay on Shatila, Genet speaks extensively of the beauty of the Palestinians, who remind him of the beauty of the Algerians when they rose against the French. He describes it as "a laughing insolence goaded by past unhappiness, systems and men responsible for unhappiness and shame, above all a laughing insolence which realizes that, freed of shame, growth is easy." The Palestinians in Gaza are beautiful. The way they care for each other in the face of death puts the rest of us to shame. Wael Dahdouh, the Al Jazeera journalist who, when his family members were killed, kept on speaking to camera, stated recently with a calm and miraculous grace: "One day this war will stop, and those of us who remain will return and rebuild, and live again in these houses."

Bibliography

Alaa Abd El-Fattah, and Naomi Klein. 2022. *You Have Not yet Been Defeated: Selected Works 2011–2021*. New York: Seven Stories Press.

Carson, Anne. "'Just for the Thrill': Sycophantizing Aristotle's 'Poetics.'" Arion: A Journal of Humanities and the Classics 1, no. 1 (1990): 142–54.

Darwish, Mahmoud. 2012. "Silence for the Sake of Gaza." *Journal of an Ordinary Grief*. Archipelago.

El-Rifae, Yasmin. 2022. *Radius*. Verso Books.

Ferrante, Elena. 2018. *My Brilliant Friend*. Book 1, the Neapolitan Novels. Melbourne, Victoria: Text Publishing Company.

Freud, Sigmund. 1974. *Moses and Monotheism: Three Essays*. London: Hogarth Press and the Institute of Psycho-Analysis.

Freud, Sigmund, and James Strachey. 2001. *Totem and Taboo and Other Works: (1913-1914)*. London: Vintage.

Genet, Jean. 1982. *4 Hours in Shatila*. Washington, DC: Institute for Palestine Studies and Kuwait University.

Ghassān Kanafānī, Barbara Harlow, and Karen E. Riley. 2000. *Palestine's Children: Returning to Haifa & Other Stories; with an Introduction and a Biographical Essay on Ghassān Kanafānī*. Boulder, Colo.: Rienner.

Gospodinov, Georgi. 2022. *Time Shelter*. Weidenfeld & Nicolson.

Kermode, Frank. 2000. *The Sense of an Ending: Studies in the Theory of Fiction*. Oxford; New York: Oxford University Press.

Levy, Deborah. 2019. *The Man Who Saw Everything*. Bloomsbury Publishing USA.

Levy, Deborah. 2023. *August Blue*. New York: Farrar, Straus and Giroux.

Levy, Deborah, Tom McCarthy, 2017. *Swimming Home*. Sheffield; London; New Haven, CT: And Other Stories.

Sven Lindqvist, and Joan Tate. 1996. *"Exterminate All the Brutes!": A Modern Odyssey into the Heart of Darkness and the Origins of European Genocide*. New York: New Press.

Javier Marías, Margaret Jull Costa, and Jonathan Coe. 2013. *A Heart so White: A Novel*. New York: Vintage International.

Nelson, Maggie. 2012. *The Art of Cruelty: A Reckoning*. New York: W.W. Norton.

Said, Edward W. 1984. "Permission to Narrate." *Journal of Palestine Studies* 13 (3): 27–48.

Said, Edward W. 2010. *The World, the Text, and the Critic*. Milton Keynes, UK; Cambridge, MA: Lightning Source UK Ltd.; Harvard University Press.

Said, Edward W. 2014. *Freud and the Non-European*. London; New York: Verso.

Wynter, Sylvia. 1971. "Novel and History, Plot and Plantation." *Savacou* 5: 95–102.